HOLT
1
FRENCH

TPR Storytelling Book

HOLT, RINEHART AND WINSTON

A Harcourt Classroom Education Company

Austin · New York · Orlando · Atlanta · San Francisco · Boston · Dallas · Toronto · London

Contributing Writers

James C. May
    Rufus King High School
    Milwaukee, WI
Carol Gaab
    Chandler, AZ

Cover Photo/Illustration Credits
Background pattern: Copyright © 1992 by Dover Publications, Inc.
Mask/Ribbons: Scott Van Osdol; teens: Marty Granger/HRW Photo

All art created by Gary Otteson.

ALLEZ, VIENS! is a trademark licensed to Holt, Rinehart and Winston, registered in the United States of America and/or other jurisdictions.

Printed in the United States of America

ISBN 0-03-065477-7

1 2 3 4 5 6 7 066 05 04 03 02 01

Contents

To the Teacher

by Carol Gaab

Total Physical Response Storytelling (TPRS) is a highly communicative methodology that promotes unrivaled fluency and lasting communication skills. Based on TPR (the single best method for long-term retention of vocabulary) and The Natural Approach, TPRS embodies sound pedagogical principles and proven elements of successful language acquisition.

A common-sense approach to learning and teaching language, TPRS facilitates a *natural* order of acquisition. While many methods focus prematurely on activities which require *output*, or production, TPRS demonstrates the need for comprehensible input (CI) to facilitate effective and rapid language acquisition. Therefore, the primary goal of the method is to provide a myriad of "input-based activities" *before* students are required to speak. Forced speech (listen and repeat) is avoided, and language learners are expected and encouraged to pass through a silent period before production takes place. The silent period simply refers to the period during which a language learner is acquiring language and gaining listening comprehension skills, but is not yet able to speak.

TPRS offers other advantages as well. Because it is a multi-sensory methodology, it meets the needs of various learning styles. Gestures and acting, for example, meet the needs of kinesthetic learners; visual images (illustrations, props, puppets, live actors, etc.) satisfy the needs of visual learners; the tremendous amount of comprehensible input not only appeals to auditory learners and compensates for those who are not auditory learners. Students develop a real "ear for the language," learning to listen and respond with what *sounds* right.

TPRS promotes skills and activities that appeal to the right hemisphere of the brain, which dominates during early stages of language acquisition. The right brain processes body language, intonation, speech melody, visual imagery, etc. These stimuli, which are inherent in TPRS, help the language learner decipher and make meaning of messages, resulting in rapid internalization, acquisition and fluency. TPRS delays (not eliminates) the introduction of discrete grammar, which is a left-brain function. This is essential to avoid a raised affective filter and a hypersensitive speech monitor, two conditions that impede acquisition and delay fluency. Subsequently, TPRS supports the rationale that linguistic accuracy is a destination, not a point of departure.

The following pages provide step-by-step instructions for successfully and easily implementing TPRS. Although it is important to complete each step, it is not necessary to do each and every activity listed within each step. Numerous suggestions are given to provide variety and avoid monotony in the classroom.

There are three basic steps to TPRS:

1. **Introduce and practice new vocabulary.**
2. **Use the new vocabulary in a story.**
3. **Revise the story and intensify acquisition.**

STEP ONE:
Introduce and practice new vocabulary.

Begin by selecting three vocabulary items from the (new) vocabulary list. New vocabulary items may consist of an individual word or an entire phrase and should be introduced and practiced in a state that is natural to speech. For example, nouns are introduced with the appropriate article, expressions and idiomatic phrases are introduced in their entirety, and verbs are introduced in a conjugated state, one verb form at a time.

Practice should begin with the present tense, 3rd person singular. After several weeks of practice when students have become proficient with that verb form, continue introducing each new verb form in the following order: third person plural, first person singular, second person, and first person plural. Finally, when introducing new verb forms and tenses, be sure to use verbs with which students are already familiar. Treat/teach (new) grammar as if it were a new vocabulary item.

Each of the three new vocabulary items should be introduced one at a time and then practiced in groups of three at a time. Say each of the three new vocabulary items (in isolation) and convey meaning through gestures, props, pictures or mini-scenarios. At times a simple illustration will suffice, but many vocabulary items will require a more in-depth explanation or if possible, a direct translation.

Once students understand the meaning of the new vocabulary item, begin teaching the associated gesture. First, say the new word or phrase and then model the appropriate gesture for your students. Second, say the new word or phrase again and model the gesture with your students. Finally, say the new word or phrase and observe your students as they do the gesture without you. Observe and assess to ensure that students know the meaning of the vocabulary item and the corresponding gesture. Then, introduce the next two vocabulary items with the same process: teach the meaning of each item and the corresponding gesture. Assess students, and when students are ready, move on to TPR practice.

The goal of TPR practice is to provide an enormous amount of comprehensible input so that students will hear each vocabulary item sixty to seventy-five times. This repetitious input is necessary for the language learner to truly internalize the vocabulary. Repeating vocabulary items sixty to seventy-five times is a challenge, but the following suggestions will make it easy, fun, and effective.

After three new vocabulary items have been introduced, practice with gestures by giving students a variety of commands that require them to respond with a specific TPR gesture. Keep in mind that the older the student, the less time will be spent on gestures. High school students will spend only an average of two to five minutes doing gestures. Use a variety of the following commands for TPR practice with gestures:

- Novel commands are commands/narrations that include new words or new combinations of words which students have not heard before. Any new or unknown word can be used for TPR practice as long as it is made comprehensible. If *(s)he is hungry, (s)he eats, the wolf* are the new vocabulary items, then have your students act out the following: *The big wolf. The small wolf. The big wolf is hungry. The big wolf is really hungry.*

- Play commands are silly commands that are intended to practice vocabulary items and to liven up a dragging or lazy class. For example, if *eats* is one of the new vocabulary items to be practiced, play commands might include the following: *Eat your big toe. Eat your nose. Eat your pencil. Eat your homework. Eat your textbook. Eat your hand.*

- Chain commands are commands/narrations that include two to three new vocabulary items at a time. For example, if *(s)he is hungry, (s)he eats, the wolf* are the new vocabulary items, these three items would be randomly combined into groups of two to three. For example, *he is hungry, he eats; he eats, he is hungry; he is hungry, he eats, the wolf; the wolf, he eats, he is hungry; the wolf, he is hungry, he eats.* Chain commands enhance long-term retention by demonstrating the power of mental imagery during the acquisition process, as students find it necessary to visualize each portion of the command in order to successfully complete it.

Practice with personalized questions and answers and personalized mini-situations. Focusing on the new vocabulary items, ask students questions that pertain to their personal experiences, likes and dislikes, and individual personalities. For example, using the three new vocabulary items *(s)he is hungry, (s)he eats, the wolf,* the following questions will help students to personally relate to the new vocabulary: *Are you hungry? Do you eat liver? What do you like to eat? Do you eat wolf?* To keep students' attention, teach to their eyes and randomly call on them to answer questions. Once questioning becomes predictable, students will pay attention only when it is their turn to answer. Make questions interesting and humorous and use students' answers as a source of information for personalized questions and answers.

The purpose of a personalized mini-situation (also referred to as a mini-scenario) is to provide more Comprehensible Input in narrative form that focuses on the new vocabulary. A personalized mini-situation should contain no more than one to three new vocabulary items and three to four basic events/ideas (not including the minor embellishments that are made as you retell it). The following is an example of a mini-scenario based on the previous three vocabulary items: *(s)he is hungry, (s)he eats, the wolf. There is a wolf. The wolf is hungry. The wolf goes to the cafeteria and sees (student in the class). The wolf eats his/her french fries. Now (student in the class) is hungry.*

The personalized mini-situation should be told and retold a number of times to ensure that students have internalized the vocabulary items and can verbalize ideas and facts about the story. Each time the mini-situation is retold, small details should be added to keep it fresh and interesting: *There is a big wolf. The wolf is very hungry. The wolf goes to the cafeteria at lunch time. The wolf sees (student in the class). (S)he has french fries. The wolf eats his/her french fries. (Student in the class) cries all afternoon. (Student in the class) is very hungry.*

The key to TPR practice is to diversify activities. In addition to the above-mentioned (TPR practice) techniques, select a variety of input-based activities, including cooperative activities and games, music and songs, or chants and rhymes. The process of introducing individual vocabulary items and practicing them in groups of three at a time is repeated until all new vocabulary items have been introduced/practiced. Once students have had ample comprehensible input (60–75 repetitions of each new vocabulary item), have learners engage in partner practice.

Partner practice is a quick and easy way for students to practice identifying and verbalizing vocabulary items. One partner says the word while the other gives the corresponding gesture. Or, one partner gives the gesture, and the other says the word. Partner practice is a highly productive cooperative learning/teaching exercise that helps students maintain a low affective filter by allowing them to work with a peer with whom they feel comfortable. Once partners have practiced all the new vocabulary items, assess their degree of acquisition.

Assessment may take a variety of forms. An easy evaluation technique is to focus on a "Barometer Student," a term invented by Blaine Ray, the innovator of TPRS. The "Barometer Student" refers to a student who is slightly below average, roughly in the fortieth percentile. The acquisition rate of a "Barometer Student" is often an ideal indicator of how to pace your class, as the rate is slow enough to keep the majority of your lower students

engaged and fast enough to avoid boring the top half of the class.

Another easy way to assess is with the "closed-eyes test." This requires students to close their eyes and respond with silent TPR as the teacher says each new vocabulary item. If 80% of the students can correctly respond to 80% of the vocabulary items, then it is safe to move on to the next step. Self assessment and partner assessment are also effective evaluation techniques. Self assessment entails simply asking students to rate themselves on a scale of one to five on their mastery/proficiency of the new vocabulary. Partner assessment requires one partner to rate the other. If more than 20% of the ratings are below a three, then more TPR practice may be required. If the assessment results are satisfactory, then it is time to move on to Step Two.

STEP TWO:
Use the vocabulary in a story.

Mini-stories give new vocabulary meaning and context, two necessary conditions for language acquisition. When introducing a mini-story, avoid "reading" a script. Know the storyline ahead of time and model good storytelling techniques, such as vocal variety, body language, and emotion for your students.

Use visuals (props, puppets, live actors, large illustrations, overhead transparencies) to accurately depict the storyline. Visuals will appeal to the right brain and long-term memory, in addition to keeping your students' attention. If live actors are used to depict the story, make sure explicit instructions are given about the emotions to be displayed, dialogue within the script, exact locations of people and places in the story, specific movements, and so on.

Successful mini-stories

- contain 6 to 12 new vocabulary items.

- are interesting.

- incorporate culture whenever possible.

- include student personalities, current or local events, responses from personalized questions and answers, known characters, such as teachers, principals, or celebrities.

- include a grammar point.

- include "sheltered" vocabulary, not "sheltered" grammar.

- contain humor and/or exaggerated details, and one silly or bizarre word.

Begin by telling the story as simply as possible. Tell and retell the story several times, adding a few minor details each time you tell it. For example, add color, size and other adjectives, adverbs, location, names, etc. Students must hear the story numerous times until they are able to retell it, making it necessary for the teacher to invent creative ways to retell the story. This is referred to as "milking" the story. There are several effective "milking" techniques.

- Ask yes/no and either/or questions.

- Tell a portion of the story and wait for students to fill in the blanks with the appropriate word or phrase.

- Ask short-answer questions.

- Make mistakes and wait for students to verbally make corrections.

- Have the class read the story from the board or overhead.

- Read various sentences from the story and have students indicate which illustration or part of the story is being described.

- Point to an illustration and have students tell that part of the story.

- Tell the story one segment at a time with no descriptions or details and have

students retell each part, adding as many descriptions and details as they are able.

Once students have heard the story numerous times, initiate a partner practice. At this stage, the purpose of partner practice is to encourage students to practice telling the mini-story in a low-stress environment. Encourage student-partners to help each other and observe as they tell the story. Walk around the room, eavesdrop on their retells, and be available to model vocabulary items, phrases and grammatical structures.

Although assessment should be a continual process, partner practice provides a good opportunity to focus on evaluating students individually. Ask students to do a self-assessment or a partner assessment and base the next step in the process on their evaluation results. If 70–80% of the students can retell 80% of the story, select a student volunteer (or student volunteers) to tell the story to the entire class. Encourage class participation by having students act out the story, provide sound effects, and be ready to provide assistance. Give positive reinforcement to any and all students who contribute to the retell!

Writing the mini-story helps students to prove just how much they have accomplished and provides an outlet to use language creatively. However, it does little to enhance language acquisition, because it is an output-based activity. Nevertheless, writing is an important skill that can easily be developed through TPRS. At what point in the process one introduces reading and writing depends on the individual teacher. Some prefer to post the written word at the time new vocabulary items are introduced. This is recommended only when dealing with literate students who have a solid knowledge of the alphabet and consonant and vowel sounds in the target language. If seeing the written word adversely affects pronunciation, then the teacher should delay showing the written word.

Assuming students have a firm foundation in the target language, the teacher can introduce the written word at any time. An effective system for beginning language learners is to verbally introduce and practice the new vocabulary. Once students have internalized the words and have developed good pronunciation, show the written vocabulary items and have students write them on flashcards or in their notebooks.

Color-coded flashcards (according to textbook chapters) provide an excellent means for recording, organizing and recycling vocabulary. Creating picture-based flashcards and dictionaries also promotes the use of visual imagery and consequently enhances long-term retention of vocabulary.

Once learners have practiced with the vocabulary in written form and they are able to retell the mini-story, it is time to begin writing it. The transition to writing is greatly simplified by doing a few of the following activities with your students first: Read the story together from the board or overhead and have students copy the sentences. Read the story sentences out of sequence and have students rewrite them in the correct order. With the entire class, read and complete a variety of extension activities, such as true-false questions, fill-in-the-blank exercises, short-answer questions and open-ended questions. These input activities will also enhance students' ability to retell the story and create revisions.

STEP THREE:
Revise the mini-story and intensify acquisition.

Creating story revisions and intensifying acquisition is the last step to TPRS. Revising stories requires the language learner to "transfer" newly acquired language to other situations and/or to creatively use it in a different context. A revision may consist of a prequel to the story (what happened before the story), a sequel (what happened after the story), an original story, a flashcard story (created from a mixture of newly acquired vocabulary and recycled vocabulary), a poem, a song, or an introduction to new grammar.

Beginning language learners typically need some direction and assistance when creating revisions, but after hearing a few teacher-generated revisions, students will soon create and retell on their own. Although they may not be able to tell a complete revision, they will provide creative ideas and details to create an entertaining revision.

Revisions provide a perfect solution for introducing new verb forms and tenses. For example, if the original vocabulary list included the verbs *he is hungry* and *he eats,* the revised vocabulary list for the revision could be converted to introduce first person singular or past tense: *I am hungry, I eat* or *he was hungry, he ate.* All grammar is treated as new vocabulary, and the entire TPRS process is repeated from the beginning. Only one verb form/tense is introduced at a time, and only mastered verbs are retaught in a new form or tense. Practice the new vocabulary (which in this case is a new verb form or tense), tell and retell the revision, and then further intensify acquisition with any of the following activities.

- Create an episode to an ongoing soap opera after each new group of vocabulary items is mastered.
- Present a related cultural lesson or a thematic unit.
- Incorporate technology with Internet research projects and Power Point® story presentations.
- Read, read, read!

When each of the three steps to the method is incorporated into the language classroom, TPRS aligns itself with the proven pedagogical principles supported by many respected experts, including Asher, Krashen, Gardner, and Hunter. It is also compatible with Bloom's Taxonomy.

- Knowledge: Knowing the literal translation of a word.
- Comprehension: Understanding meaning and how/when vocabulary is used.
- Application: Being able to use vocabulary appropriately in a story.
- Analysis: The ability to determine appropriate social setting and context.
- Synthesis: Creative use of vocabulary; circumlocution.
- Evaluation: Revising, editing, paraphrasing, rewording.

Each step follows a logical and pedagogically sound sequence. By following each one, you will ensure that essential conditions are met for successful, rapid, and lasting language acquisition.

Faisons connaissance!
PREMIERE ETAPE

Vocabulaire

Bonjour.

Je m'appelle…

J'ai 14 ans.

Moi, ça va très bien.

Elle s'appelle…

Elle a 15 ans.

J'adore…

Tchao.

Mini-histoire

Bonjour! Je m'appelle Thomas. J'ai 14 ans. Moi, ça va très bien. Et elle, elle s'appelle Julie. Elle a 15 ans. J'adore Julie! Tchao!

Faisons connaissance!
DEUXIEME ETAPE

Vocabulaire

dit
J'aime…
le football
Je n'aime pas…

Je préfère…
le ski
les frites
J'aime mieux…

les escargots
J'aime bien…
le cinéma
la plage

Mini-histoire

Thomas dit à Julie, «J'aime le football.» Julie dit, «Je n'aime pas le football. Je préfère le ski.» Thomas dit, «J'adore les frites.» Julie dit, «Je n'aime pas les frites. J'aime mieux les escargots.» Thomas dit, «J'aime bien le cinéma.» Julie dit, «Je n'aime pas le cinéma. J'aime la plage. Au revoir!» Pauvre Thomas!

Faisons connaissance!
TROISIEME ETAPE

Vocabulaire

regarder la télé   danser   parler au téléphone

aussi   dormir   est triste

écouter de la musique   étudier

Mini-histoire

Thomas aime regarder la télé. Il aime aussi écouter de la musique. Il
aime bien danser et il adore dormir. Il n'aime pas étudier. Il adore parler
au téléphone avec Julie, mais Julie n'aime pas parler avec Thomas. Thomas
est triste.

PREMIERE ETAPE

TPRS Gestures

Bonjour. wave hello

Je m'appelle... point to yourself and say your name

J'ai 14 ans. point to yourself, hold up fingers on hand twice, then the third time only hold up 4 fingers

Moi, ça va très bien. point to yourself, have a big smile on face

Elle s'appelle... point to a girl in class and say her name

Elle a 15 ans. point to a girl in class, hold up all fingers on hand three times

J'adore... pound fist on heart three times

Tchao. wave goodbye over shoulder

Teaching Suggestions

- Have students substitute their own age and name when retelling the story. You might also have them use the name of a celebrity instead of "Julie."

- Students might also continue the story by having Thomas ask Julie how she is feeling.

Additional Vocabulary

Il s'appelle... point to a boy in class and say his name

Au revoir. same gesture as **Tchao**

Comment ça va? mime shaking someone's hand

DEUXIEME ETAPE

TPRS Gestures

dit touch lips with fingers and pull fingers away to represent speech

J'aime... hand over heart

le football mime bouncing soccer ball on knee

Je n'aime pas... same gesture as **J'aime,** but shake head no

Je préfère... show two pictures of different foods (chocolate cake versus brussel sprouts, for example) and point to the one you prefer

le ski mime snowskiing

les frites mime eating French fries one at a time, holding "box" in other hand

J'aime mieux... same gesture as **je préfère**

les escargots draw shape of snails in air

J'aime bien... pound hand on heart two times

le cinéma point to name of a movie theater on board

la plage mime putting on sunblock

Teaching Suggestions

- Explain to students the meaning of **Pauvre Thomas!** before you present the story.

- Allow students to suggest alternate gestures where there is a chance for personalization. For example, some students may associate the beach more with playing volleyball than with putting on sunblock.

Additional Vocabulary

les vacances put clasped hands behind head and lean back

l'école write the name of a school on the board and point to it

le français point to French textbook

l'anglais point to English textbook

TROISIEME ETAPE

TPRS Gestures

regarder la télé pretend to "channel surf" with remote

aussi tap two index fingers against each other two times

écouter de la musique point to ears and then bob head as if listening to music

danser dance around

dormir close eyes and snore

étudier mime studying a book

parler au téléphone mime talking on the telephone

est triste make a sad face by pulling down corners of mouth

Teaching Suggestions

- Give students the definition of **avec** before you present the story.

- When students tell the story, allow them to change the story as they like as long as the context makes sense. **Danser** could be interchanged with **dormir,** and so on.

Additional Vocabulary

nager mime swimming

lire mime reading by looking at two open hands touching

voyager mime carrying a suitcase

faire le ménage mime dusting off desk

Vive l'école!
PREMIERE ETAPE

Vocabulaire

la biologie   l'algèbre   l'informatique
Moi, non.   Moi, pas trop.   les devoirs
la chimie   le sport

Mini-histoire

Salut! Je m'appelle François. Tu aimes la biologie? Moi, non, mais j'aime bien la chimie. Tu aimes l'algèbre? Moi, pas trop. Tu aimes le sport? Moi, j'adore le sport et l'informatique aussi. Et j'aime les devoirs—avec les hamburgers et les frites!

Vive l'école!
DEUXIEME ETAPE

Vocabulaire

aujourd'hui
samedi
le matin
a deux cours

à neuf heures
à dix heures quinze
l'après-midi

contente
demain
dimanche

Mini-histoire

Aujourd'hui, c'est samedi. Le matin, Suzanne a deux cours. Elle a maths à neuf heures. Elle a chimie à dix heures quinze. L'après-midi, Suzanne regarde la télévision. Elle est contente. Demain, c'est dimanche. Suzanne adore le dimanche!

Vive l'école!
TROISIEME ETAPE

Vocabulaire

C'est difficile.	C'est super!	C'est génial!
C'est intéressant.	C'est cool.	C'est passionnant!

Mini-histoire

Marie n'aime pas la biologie. C'est difficile. Elle aime bien les maths. C'est intéressant. L'histoire, c'est super! Le français, c'est cool. L'espagnol, c'est génial! Mais Marie adore l'anglais. C'est passionnant! Jérôme est dans la classe d'anglais!

Teacher Notes

PREMIERE ETAPE

TPRS Gestures

la biologie mime looking through a microscope

Moi, non. point to yourself, shake head no

la chimie mime pouring liquid from a beaker into a test tube

l'algèbre point to an algebra problem written on the board

Moi, pas trop. point to yourself and move hand back and forth to mean "so-so"

le sport hold up a picture of a sports magazine or point to pictures of different sports

l'informatique mime using keyboard and mouse

les devoirs hold up a notebook

Teaching Suggestions

• Have students retell the story using their own class schedules.

• After students retell the story, have them write a response to François. Have students agree and disagree with his opinions of his classes.

Additional Vocabulary

la physique point to physics book or a physics problem written on the board

la géométrie point to a geometry problem written on the board or to geometry book

la musique sing "la-la-la" and mime playing piano

DEUXIEME ETAPE

TPRS Gestures

aujourd'hui point to today's date written on the board or calendar

samedi point to Saturday on calendar

le matin stretch like you just woke up

a deux cours point to names of subjects on board and hold up two fingers

à neuf heures point to 9:00 on a clock drawn on board

à dix heures quinze point to 10:15 on a clock drawn on board

l'après-midi have arm and hand turned down, outstretched, and lower hand slowly to symbolize sun going down

contente raise corners of mouth and put thumb on chin

demain point to tomorrow's date written on the board or calendar

dimanche point to Sunday on calendar

Teaching Suggestions

• Explain to students that students in France usually go to school on Saturday morning.

• You might tell students that **le dimanche** means *Sundays* (in general).

• Have students retell the first part of the story using two students, so they can practice different forms of **avoir.**

Additional Vocabulary

maintenant point index finger down to symbolize "right now"

TROISIEME ETAPE

TPRS Gestures

C'est difficile. scrape knuckles together to indicate the concept of something difficult

C'est intéressant. rub chin with thumb and index finger and say "hmmm"

C'est super! hold arms up in air

C'est cool! hold one thumb up

C'est génial! hold two thumbs up

C'est passionnant! extend both hands up, palms open, and move hands slightly back and forth

Teaching Suggestions

• You might give students the meaning of **dans** before you present the story.

• If you present the expression **C'est barbant** from the Additional Vocabulary below, explain to students that this is a gesture used by the French to express boredom.

• Have students retell the story using their own classes and opinions.

Additional Vocabulary

C'est facile. lightly touch fingertips on one hand with those of another

C'est zéro. make "zero" with fingers and thumb

C'est pas terrible. motion hand in a "so-so" gesture

C'est pas super. throw hand forward and shake head no

C'est barbant. rub side of face with back of hand where a beard would normally be

C'est nul. pretend to push something off desk to show it's worthless

Tout pour la rentrée
PREMIÈRE ÉTAPE

Vocabulaire

le sac à dos   des stylos   un taille-crayon
une trousse   une gomme   un classeur
une calculatrice un livre   un crayon

Mini-histoire

Dans le sac à dos de Caroline, il y a une trousse, une calculatrice, des stylos, une gomme, six livres, un taille-crayon et deux classeurs. Karim a aussi un sac à dos. Dans le sac à dos de Karim, il y a un crayon et... du chocolat!

Tout pour la rentrée
DEUXIEME ETAPE

Vocabulaire

Il voudrait acheter…   ce jean   vert(s)/verte(s)
ces baskets   bleu(s)/bleue(s)   ce disque compact
noir(s)/noire(s)   cette montre   cet ordinateur
blanc(s)/blanche(s)

Mini-histoire

Serge est dans un magasin. Il voudrait acheter ces baskets noires et blanches.
Il voudrait acheter ce jean bleu et ce jean noir aussi. Serge adore faire les
magasins! Il voudrait aussi acheter cette montre verte, ce disque compact et
cet ordinateur, mais il a seulement huit euros. Il est triste.

Tout pour la rentrée
TROISIÈME ÉTAPE

Vocabulaire

Pardon.	90
C'est combien?	140
répond	Merci.

Mini-histoire

Marie-Claire est dans un magasin. Elle dit, «Pardon, monsieur. Ce portefeuille bleu, c'est combien?» M. Martin répond, «90 euros.» Marie-Claire dit, «Et ce portefeuille blanc, c'est combien?» M. Martin répond, «140 euros.» Marie-Claire dit, «Merci, monsieur, mais il me faut un portefeuille noir!» M. Martin n'est pas content.

Teacher Notes

PREMIERE ETAPE

TPRS Gestures

le sac à dos touch back and point to backpack

une trousse mime zipping up pencil case

une calculatrice mime holding calculator and pushing buttons

des stylos hold up or point to some pens

une gomme hold up or point to eraser

un livre put both hands together; then open them, keeping little fingers together as if opening a book

un taille-crayon mime sharpening pencil

un classeur mime pulling apart binder rings with index fingers

un crayon hold up or point to pencil

Teaching Suggestions

- Give students the definition of **dans** and **il y a** before you present the story.

- You might use actual classroom items to present the story.

Additional Vocabulary

des feuilles de papier hold up or point to pieces of paper

un cahier hold up or point to notebook

une règle hold up index fingers about a foot apart and make shape of a ruler

DEUXIEME ETAPE

TPRS Gestures

Il voudrait acheter... mime counting money out for a cashier, smiling

ces baskets point to athletic shoes

noir(s)/noire(s) point to or hold up black piece of paper

blanc(s)/blanche(s) point to or hold up white piece of paper

ce jean point to jeans

bleu(s)/bleue(s) point to or hold up blue piece of paper

cette montre touch watch or tap wrist with index finger to show where watch would be

vert(s)/verte(s) point to or hold up green piece of paper

ce disque compact approximate the size of a CD with hands and then mime listening to music

cet ordinateur point to computer in classroom or drawing on board

Teaching Suggestions

- Give students the definition of **seulement** before presenting the story. You might also remind them that **triste** means *sad*.

- Tell students beforehand how the value of the franc compares to the dollar, doing some quick conversion problems to make sure students understand. You might also use the euro as the currency.

- You might switch items and colors when retelling the story so students have more practice with adjective agreement.

- You might add **ce jean-là** to the story so students can see the contrast with adding **là**.

Additional Vocabulary

ce short use hands to mark place on leg where shorts would end and make chopping motion against leg

ce roman point to novel

ce portefeuille touch pocket or purse where one would normally carry a wallet or mime opening a wallet

TROISIEME ETAPE

TPRS Gestures

Pardon. mime getting someone's attention by tapping them on the shoulder

C'est combien? point to price tag with question mark on it

répond touch fingers to lips, pull fingers away, and bring fingers back to lips

90 show nine fingers, then make a "0" with fingers

140 once make a letter "C" once with fingers ("C" is the Roman numeral for one hundred.) then show four fingers and then make a "0" with the fingers

Merci. move tips of fingers away from mouth, almost like you're throwing someone a kiss to say "thank you"

Teaching Suggestion

- You should have a price tag drawn on the board or transparency with a question mark on it.

Additional Vocabulary

Excusez-moi. same gesture as **pardon**

60 show six fingers, then make a "0" with the fingers

80 show eight fingers, then make a "0" with the fingers

Sports et passe-temps
PREMIERE ETAPE

Vocabulaire

jouer au foot

pas tellement

faire du roller en ligne

pas beaucoup

faire des photos

pas du tout

faire du jogging

jouer à des jeux vidéo

faire un pique-nique

beaucoup

manger

Mini-histoire

Après l'école, est-ce que Nicolas aime jouer au foot? Pas tellement. Il aime faire du roller en ligne? Pas beaucoup. Il aime faire des photos? Pas du tout. Il aime faire du jogging? Non, pas beaucoup. Il aime jouer à des jeux vidéo? Non, pas tellement. Il aime faire un pique-nique? Oui, beaucoup! Nicolas adore manger!

Sports et passe-temps
DEUXIEME ETAPE

Vocabulaire

Qu'est-ce que tu fais comme sport?

au printemps

il pleut

en été

il fait chaud

en automne

il fait frais

en hiver

il fait froid

il neige

Mini-histoire

Qu'est-ce que tu fais comme sport? Marc adore jouer au base-ball. Il joue au base-ball au printemps, quand il pleut. Il joue au base-ball en été, quand il fait chaud. Il joue au base-ball en automne, quand il fait frais. Il joue au base-ball en hiver, quand il fait froid et quand il neige. Et pourquoi? Mais parce qu'il adore jouer au base-ball!

Sports et passe-temps
TROISIEME ETAPE

Vocabulaire

demande

On fait du patin à glace?

Désolé(e), mais je ne peux pas.

On joue au basket?

jamais

On fait du vélo?

Ça ne me dit rien.

On fait de l'aérobic?

Bonne idée!

Mini-histoire

Serge parle à Suzanne. Elle demande, «On fait du patin à glace?» Serge répond, «Désolé, mais je ne peux pas.» Suzanne demande, «On joue au basket?» Serge répond, «Non, je ne joue jamais au basket.» Suzanne demande, «On fait du vélo?» Serge répond, «Ça ne me dit rien.» Suzanne dit, «On fait de l'aérobic?» Serge répond, «Bonne idée! Et on mange des frites, du chocolat et de la glace après?»

PREMIERE ETAPE

TPRS Gestures

jouer au foot mime kicking soccer ball with foot

pas tellement make "so-so" gesture with hand and shake head no

faire du roller en ligne mime doing in-line skating

pas beaucoup same gesture as **pas tellement**

faire des photos mime taking a picture of someone

pas du tout shake head no aggressively

faire du jogging mime jogging, pumping arms at side

jouer à des jeux vidéo mime playing video game using joystick

faire un pique-nique mime spreading blanket on floor and opening picnic basket

beaucoup gesture "a lot of" with hands

manger mime chewing

Teaching Suggestions

• Give students the definition of **après** before telling the story.

• Allow students to show you a gesture they associate with a certain activity or sport. For example, let them show you the gesture they associate with **jouer à des jeux vidéo** and then use that gesture.

• Students might prefer to stand while they make the gestures for this lesson.

Additional Vocabulary

faire du ski nautique mime holding a water-ski rope and lean back

jouer au volley(-ball) mime playing volleyball

jouer au base-ball mime holding baseball bat and swing

jouer au tennis mime hitting ball with tennis racket

DEUXIEME ETAPE

TPRS Gestures

Qu'est-ce que tu fais comme sport? point to cluster of sports and a question mark written together on blackboard

au printemps mime taking a stroll and smelling flowers

il pleut mime holding umbrella

en été make a sun with both hands above head and squint to show it's bright

il fait chaud mime wiping sweat off forehead

en automne make an outline of leaf with hand, then make downward motion with hand to represent leaves falling

il fait frais rub arms lightly as if trying to warm up

en hiver pretend to shiver

il fait froid rub hands together as if cold

il neige move both hands downward while wiggling fingers to represent snow falling

Teaching Suggestion

• Give students the definition of **pourquoi, parce que,** and **quand** before telling the story.

Additional Vocabulary

il fait beau sweep hand through the air in the shape of an arc with fingers apart to represent a rainbow

TROISIEME ETAPE

TPRS Gestures

demande make talking gesture with hand, then make question mark in air

On fait du patin à glace? mime ice skating

Désolé(e), mais je ne peux pas. make fist, "pound" against heart at least twice, and shake head no

On joue au basket? mime shooting (or dribbling) a basketball

jamais make "time out" sign and shake head no

On fait du vélo? mime holding onto bicycle handlebars and lean body forwards

Ça ne me dit rien. make a zero with hand, then move hand away while spreading fingers

On fait de l'aérobic? mime doing a jumping jack

Bonne idée! put index finger to temple of head, then pull finger up and out

Teaching Suggestion

• Before presenting the gestures for the questions above, make a question mark in the air.

Additional Vocabulary

D'accord. hold thumb up and wink

Allons-y! point to door with both index fingers, motioning to "come on"

On va au café?
PREMIERE ETAPE

Vocabulaire

J'ai faim.

On va au café?

prendre

un sandwich au jambon

Désolé(e).

J'ai des devoirs à faire.

J'ai des trucs à faire.

J'ai des tas de choses à faire.

chez Fatima

Mini-histoire

Jacques parle à Karim. Jacques dit, «J'ai faim. On va au café pour prendre un sandwich au jambon?» Karim répond, «Désolé. J'ai des devoirs à faire.» Jacques demande, «On fait du roller en ligne?» Karim répond, «Désolé. J'ai des trucs à faire.» Jacques demande, «On joue au basket?» Karim répond, «Désolé. J'ai des tas de choses à faire.» Jacques dit, «On va chez Fatima?» Karim répond, «Bonne idée! Allons-y!» Karim est très content.

On va au café?
DEUXIEME ETAPE

Vocabulaire

le serveur

Excusez-moi…

Monsieur!

La carte, s'il vous plaît!

Vous prenez?

Je voudrais…

Je vais prendre…

la boisson

Apportez-moi…

Donnez-moi…

Mini-histoire

Dominique est au café. Elle dit au serveur, «Excusez-moi, monsieur! La carte, s'il vous plaît!» Le serveur demande, «Vous prenez?» Dominique répond, «Je voudrais un hamburger. Et je vais prendre un steak-frites, s'il vous plaît. Et comme boisson, apportez-moi une limonade et un coca… Et donnez-moi un hot-dog, s'il vous plaît. Et je voudrais aussi de la glace.» Dominique a très faim!

On va au café?
TROISIEME ETAPE

Vocabulaire

C'est combien,... ?   C'est pas terrible.
C'est (2) euros (90).   C'est dégoûtant.
C'est pas bon.   C'est excellent.

Mini-histoire

Emilie est au café. Elle demande, «C'est combien, un sandwich au jambon?»
Le serveur répond, «C'est deux euros quatre-vingt-dix.» Elle dit, «Je n'aime
pas le jambon. C'est pas bon. C'est combien, une pizza?» Le serveur répond,
«C'est trois euros cinq.» Emilie dit, «Je n'aime pas le fromage. C'est pas
terrible. C'est combien, un hamburger?» Le serveur répond, «C'est trois euros
trente-cinq.» Elle dit, «Je n'aime pas les hamburgers. C'est dégoûtant. C'est
combien, un café?» Le serveur répond, «C'est un euro vingt-deux.» Emilie dit,
«J'aime bien le café. C'est excellent! Donnez-moi un café, s'il vous plaît.»
Emilie est contente, mais le serveur n'est pas content!

PREMIERE ETAPE

TPRS Gestures

J'ai faim. rub stomach

On va au café? mime sipping a cup of coffee

prendre hold hands out, make grasping motion, and pull hands back

un sandwich au jambon mime putting meat on slice of bread and topping meat with another slice of bread

Désolé(e). hang head shamefully, shake head no

J'ai des devoirs à faire. hold up a notebook and mime writing in it

J'ai des trucs à faire. extend both index fingers and "roll" them around each other slowly.

J'ai des tas de choses à faire. same gesture as **J'ai des trucs à faire** but "roll" fingers around each other faster

chez Fatima make "roof" of house with two middle fingers touching and point to Fatima's name written on the board

Teaching Suggestion

- Allow students to give Karim's excuses in any order as long as they understand what they are saying.

Additional Vocabulary

J'ai soif. hold throat and open mouth

un hot-dog mime holding hot dog and taking a bite

une omelette mime cracking eggs and whipping them

un jus d'orange mime squeezing an orange and drinking

DEUXIEME ETAPE

TPRS Gestures

le serveur mime carrying a tray with one hand

Excusez-moi... raise index finger and shake it a little as if trying to get someone's attention

Monsieur! raise index finger and hold hand up high, as if calling for a waiter in a restaurant

La carte, s'il vous plaît! same gesture as **Monsieur!**, then take index finger and lower it in front of you, as if reading a menu

Vous prenez? point to three food items and question marks written closely together on the chalkboard

Je voudrais... point to one thing you would like from the group of foods listed on the board

Je vais prendre... run finger over menu, stop at a certain item, and point

la boisson mime drinking a beverage

Apportez-moi... move open hand towards body, as if gesturing to someone to bring you something

Donnez-moi... point index finger away from body, then towards body, as if gesturing to someone to give you something

Teaching Suggestion

- Encourage students to add more food items to Dominique's order once they know the basic story. You might also encourage students to come up with unique food combinations.

Additional Vocabulary

Qu'est-ce que vous avez comme sandwiches? make question mark in the air and point to **au fromage** and **au jambon** written on the board

Qu'est-ce qu'il y a comme boissons? make question mark in the air and point to **coca** and **jus de pomme** written on the board

Vous avez choisi? same gesture as **Vous prenez?**

TROISIEME ETAPE

TPRS Gestures

C'est combien,... ? point to price tag with question mark on it

C'est (2) euros quatre-vingt-dix. point to "2,90 €" (or other prices) written on the board

C'est pas bon. shake head indicating "no" while you're frowning

C'est pas terrible. wrinkle your nose and shake head indicating "no"

C'est dégoûtant. stick out tongue and have a disgusted look on your face

C'est excellent. hold two thumbs up

Teaching Suggestion

- The items and prices in the story are taken from the menu on page 156 of the *Pupil's Edition.* You might refer students to the menus on pages 158 and 159 if you have them invent their own stories.

Additional Vocabulary

C'est bon! rub stomach and smile

C'est délicieux! lick lips

Oui, tout de suite. snap fingers several times

Amusons-nous!
PREMIERE ETAPE

Vocabulaire

Qu'est-ce que Fatou va faire ce week-end?

voir un match de football

au stade

faire un pique-nique

faire les vitrines

au centre commercial

aller à une boum

faire une promenade

au parc

être fatigué(e)

Mini-histoire

Qu'est-ce que Fatou va faire ce week-end? Samedi matin, elle va voir un match de football au stade. Samedi après-midi, elle va faire un pique-nique et faire les vitrines au centre commercial. Et samedi soir, elle va aller à une boum. Dimanche, elle veut faire une promenade au parc, mais elle va être très fatiguée! Elle va dormir dimanche matin, dimanche après-midi et dimanche soir!

Amusons-nous!
DEUXIEME ETAPE

Vocabulaire

Allons…

Ça ne me dit rien.

Tu veux aller au café avec moi?

J'ai des trucs à faire.

Tu viens?

Désolé(e), je ne peux pas.

Je veux bien.

Mini-histoire

Cédric dit à Annie, «Allons au parc!» Elle répond, «Ça ne me dit rien.» Cédric demande à Alain, «Tu veux aller au café avec moi?» Alain répond, «J'ai des trucs à faire.» Cédric demande à Sophie, «Je voudrais aller au cinéma. Tu viens?» Sophie répond, «Désolée, je ne peux pas.» Cédric dit à sa maman, «Allons faire du vélo.» Et sa mère répond, «Oui, je veux bien!» La mère de Cédric est super!

Vocabulaire

Quand?   A quelle heure?

Ce week-end.   A sept heures et demie.

On se retrouve où?   Bon.

devant   rendez-vous

Mini-histoire

Robert dit à Karine, «Tu veux aller au cinéma avec moi?» Karine demande, «Quand?» Robert répond, «Ce week-end.» Elle demande, «On se retrouve où?» Robert dit, «Devant le café.» Karine dit «A quelle heure?» Il dit, «A sept heures et demie.» Karine dit, «D'accord!» Robert dit, «Bon, rendez-vous samedi soir, devant le café.» Karine répond, «Oh! Pas samedi soir! J'ai rendez-vous avec David!»

Teacher Notes

PREMIERE ETAPE

TPRS Gestures

Qu'est-ce que Fatou va faire ce week-end? make question mark in the air, then point to a weekend on a calendar

voir un match de football point to eye while miming kicking a soccer ball

au stade do "the wave" as they do in large games

faire un pique-nique mime spreading blanket on floor and opening picnic basket

faire les vitrines point to eye and say name of local department store

au centre commercial point to name of local mall on board

aller à une boum dance around, pretend to chat with friends

faire une promenade walk around

au parc mime sitting on a park bench, looking at sun

être fatigué(e) yawn and stretch arms

Teaching Suggestions

• Encourage students to change some of the weekend activities when they retell the story.

• Have students retell the story using Fatou and a friend. Remind students to make all the necessary changes. (**Dimanche, ils vont...**)

Additional Vocabulary

voir un film point to screen in room

manger quelque chose mime eating and sipping beverage

Rien de spécial. brush something away

Pas grand-chose. same gesture as **Rien de spécial.**

voir une pièce point to a book of a famous play displayed in chalkboard tray

DEUXIEME ETAPE

TPRS Gestures

Allons... gesture as if calling someone over

Ça ne me dit rien. make a zero, then move hand away while spreading fingers

Tu veux aller au café avec moi? make question mark in the air, point to a student, and mime sipping coffee

J'ai des trucs à faire. extend index fingers and roll them around each other slowly

Tu viens? bend arm at elbow with index finger extended, then bring hand up, pointing to self

Désolé(e), je ne peux pas. make fist, "pound" against heart twice, and shake head no

Je veux bien. shake head yes rapidly

Teaching Suggestions

• Give students the definition of **mère** before presenting the story.

• Before presenting this vocabulary, you might review the expressions for making suggestions and excuses presented in Chapters 4 and 5.

Additional Vocabulary

d'accord hold thumb up

Pourquoi pas? raise shoulders, extend hands with palms up, and raise eyebrows

Désolé(e), je suis occupé(e). shake head no and then pretend to write something using index finger

TROISIEME ETAPE

TPRS Gestures

Quand? make question mark in the air and point to different days on calendar

Ce week-end. point to Saturday and Sunday on calendar

On se retrouve où? extend one index finger and make circular motion in the air

devant hold hand (sideways and open palm) in front of you

A quelle heure? make question mark in the air and point to watch on wrist

A sept heures et demie. draw clock on board showing 7:30

Bon. hold one thumb up

rendez-vous start with index fingers apart, then gradually move them together to represent two people meeting

Teaching Suggestions

• Review telling time before presenting the story. Students might change the times when they retell the story.

• You might give students a copy of a calendar page, so they can point to the days easily while remaining at their own desks.

Additional Vocabulary

Quand ça? same gesture as **Quand?**

Tout de suite. snap fingers once

Entendu. point to ear and nod

La famille
PREMIERE ETAPE

Vocabulaire

Comment est la famille de... ?
le père
la mère
le frère
la sœur

l'oncle
la tante
le cousin
la cousine

le chien
le chat
le canari
le poisson

Mini-histoire

Comment est la famille de Patricia? Elle a un père et une mère. Elle a six frères et cinq sœurs, quatre oncles et cinq tantes. Elle a dix cousins et onze cousines. Et elle a cinq chiens, six chats, sept canaris et huit poissons. Comment est sa famille? Grande!

La famille
DEUXIEME ETAPE

Vocabulaire

Il est comment?	intelligent(e)	timide
brun(e)	sympathique	petit(e)
grand(e)	un peu	pénible

❶

❷

❸

❹

Mini-histoire

Etienne est le frère de Denise. Il est comment? Il est brun, grand, intelligent, sympathique et un peu timide. Denise est brune, petite et intelligente. Mais elle est aussi pénible; elle adore manger des frites, surtout les frites de son frère!

La famille
TROISIEME ETAPE

Vocabulaire

faire le ménage
ranger sa chambre
tondre le gazon

garder sa petite sœur
débarrasser la table
promener le chien

sortir la poubelle
laver la voiture

①

vendredi	samedi	dimanche
5	6	7
12	13	14
19	20	21

Mini-histoire

C'est le week-end, mais Philippe ne veut pas aller au cinéma. Il ne veut
pas jouer au foot. Samedi, il veut faire le ménage. Il veut ranger sa chambre,
tondre le gazon et garder sa petite sœur. Dimanche, il veut débarrasser la
table, promener le chien, sortir la poubelle et laver la voiture. Philippe est
intéressant, n'est-ce pas?

Teacher Notes

PREMIERE ETAPE

TPRS Gestures

Comment est la famille de... ? make question mark in air, point to family tree on board or to a picture of a family

le père touch forehead with thumb

la mère touch chin with thumb

le frère touch forehead with thumb, then lower thumb to about chest level to represent a younger male

la sœur touch chin with thumb, then lower thumb to about chest level to represent a younger female

l'oncle form the letter "O" with hand and place on forehead

la tante form the letter "T" with hands and place on chin

le cousin form the letter "C" with hand and place on forehead

la cousine form the letter "C" with hand and place on chin

le chien pat hand on leg as if calling a dog

le chat mime stroking "cat whiskers" on face

le canari extend the thumb and index finger in front of mouth and open and close fingers to represent a bird's beak

le poisson place open hand in front of body and zig-zag to imitate a fish swimming

Teaching Suggestions

- Tell students that in general, American Sign Language refers to a male with a sign above the nose and to a female with one below the nose.

- You may want to prepare a family tree for the class to point to or use the family tree on page 204 of the *Pupil's Edition.*

- Before presenting the story, you might review numbers with students. You might also give them the definition of **grande.**

Additional Vocabulary

le mari touch forehead with thumb, then point to ring finger

la femme touch chin with thumb, then point to ring finger

le fils touch forehead with thumb, then make a rocking motion with both arms (represents rocking a son to sleep)

la fille touch chin with thumb, then make a rocking motion with both arms (represents rocking a daughter to sleep)

DEUXIEME ETAPE

TPRS Gestures

Il est comment? point to **blond/gros/petit** and question marks written on chalkboard

brun(e) point to dark-haired male student and female student respectively

grand(e) hold hand far above head

intelligent(e) touch both temples of the head and mime studying

sympathique stroke hand

un peu show a "little bit" with fingers

timide put finger on lip and look down

petit(e) put open hand parallel to floor (hand should be close to floor to approximate "small")

pénible rub neck with hand to symbolize "a pain in the neck"

Teaching Suggestion

- Repeat the gestures for the adjectives several times with both male and female students so students can hear the difference in the forms.

Additional Vocabulary

blond(e) point to blond-haired male or female student

amusant(e) hold stomach and laugh

fort(e) flex muscle

TROISIEME ETAPE

TPRS Gestures

faire le ménage mime dusting off desk

ranger sa chambre mime making bed and putting things away

tondre le gazon mime pushing lawnmower

garder sa petite sœur mime patting young person on the head

débarrasser la table mime taking dishes off table

promener le chien mime walking dog on leash

sortir la poubelle hold nose and pretend to carry a trash bag

laver la voiture mime washing car

Teaching Suggestion

- Tell students what **n'est-ce pas** means before telling the story.

Additional Vocabulary

passer l'aspirateur mime vacuuming

faire la vaisselle mime washing dishes

Au marché
PREMIERE ETAPE

Vocabulaire

un supermarché	une tomate	un poulet
a besoin de	du pain	une tarte
de (la) salade	du beurre	un gâteau
une banane		

Mini-histoire

Ousmane va au supermarché. Sa mère a besoin de salade, de bananes, de tomates, de pain, de beurre et de poulet. Il y a de la salade, mais Ousmane n'achète pas de salade. Il n'achète pas de bananes, de tomates, de beurre, de pain ni de poulet non plus! Qu'est-ce qu'il achète? Une tarte et un gâteau. Sa mère n'est pas contente!

Au marché
DEUXIEME ETAPE

Vocabulaire

Tu peux aller faire les courses?
Bon, d'accord.
J'y vais tout de suite.

une boîte de
un paquet de
une douzaine de

un morceau de
un kilo de
malade

Mini-histoire

Ousmane parle avec sa mère. Elle dit, «Tu peux aller faire les courses?»
Ousmane dit, «Bon, d'accord. J'y vais tout de suite.» Ousmane achète une
boîte de tomates, un paquet de sucre, une douzaine d'œufs, un morceau
de fromage et un kilo d'oignons. Mais Ousmane a très faim! Il mange les
tomates, le sucre, les œufs, le fromage et les oignons! Maintenant il n'a
pas très faim; il est très malade!

Au marché
TROISIEME ETAPE

Vocabulaire

dîne	Tu prends… ?	Je n'ai plus faim.
Tu veux… ?	Non, merci.	Oui, s'il te plaît.
Je n'en veux plus.	Encore… ?	J'en veux bien.

Mini-histoire

Laurent dîne avec sa mère. Elle dit, «Tu veux du chocolat?» Laurent répond, «Non, je n'en veux plus.» Sa mère demande, «Tu prends de la glace?» Il dit, «Non, merci.» Sa mère demande, «Encore du fromage?» Il répond, «Non, merci. Je n'ai plus faim.» Sa mère demande, «Tu veux des petits pois?» Il répond, «Oui, s'il te plaît, Maman. J'en veux bien.» Laurent adore les petits pois!

PREMIERE ETAPE

TPRS Gestures

un supermarché mime pushing a shopping cart

a besoin de hold both hands extended in front, clasp hands together and bring to heart

de (la) salade mime shredding lettuce and tossing a salad

une banane hold up index finger and mime "peeling" it

une tomate mime cutting tomatoes

du pain mime slicing bread and making a sandwich

du beurre mime cutting butter and buttering bread

un poulet flap arms with bent elbows

une tarte open palm of one hand and pretend there is a small pie in the palm of your hand, then take other hand and mime cutting the pie into wedges

un gâteau mime blowing out candles on a cake

Teaching Suggestions

• Tell students what **ne... ni...** means before presenting the story.

• Tell students what **non plus** means before presenting the story.

Additional Vocabulary

du lait mime milking a cow with two hands

des petits pois extend index finger to represent a pea pod, then mime pointing to the peas in the pod

des œufs mime cracking eggs

du maïs mime eating corn on the cob

DEUXIEME ETAPE

TPRS Gestures

Tu peux aller faire les courses? mime taking food items off supermarket shelf and putting them in a shopping cart

Bon, d'accord. nod, hold thumb up

J'y vais tout de suite. point towards door, then snap fingers

une boîte de mime opening can with can opener

un paquet de mime tearing off top of sack/carton

une douzaine de show all ten fingers and then two more

un morceau de approximate small quantity with thumb and index finger

un kilo de hold hand open and push up one time to represent "one" kilo or mime scales with hands

malade hold stomach and have sick look on face

Teaching Suggestion

• Encourage students to make food substitutions, like **une boîte de maïs** in place of **une boîte de tomates**.

Additional Vocabulary

une bouteille de mime drinking out of bottle

une tranche de mime slicing something with hand vertically in air

Je veux bien. nod head "yes" and hold both thumbs up

Rapporte-moi... open hand in front of yourself; then bring hand towards yourself to represent "bring back"

TROISIEME ETAPE

TPRS Gestures

dîne mime eating and then lower arm to represent the sun going down

Tu veux... ? use index finger to point to imaginary item, raise eyebrows to indicate a question

Je n'en veux plus. mime pushing food away

Tu prends... ? same gesture as **Tu veux... ?**

Non, merci. shake head no and hold hand up as if to "block" more food

Encore... ? offer someone more food

Je n'ai plus faim. pat stomach and shake head no

Oui, s'il te plaît. put hands together as if pleading for something

J'en veux bien. shake head yes while holding out plate

Teaching Suggestion

• You might change the food Laurent loves each time you tell the story.

Additional Vocabulary

le petit déjeuner mime eating and then raise hand to represent the sun rising

le déjeuner mime eating and then raise arm to shoulder to represent 12:00 noon

le goûter mime eating peanuts, a candy bar, or some sort of snack

Au téléphone
PREMIERE ETAPE

Vocabulaire

d'abord	après	finalement
a fait ses devoirs	a lu	a raté le bus
ensuite	est allé	a passé un très mauvais week-end
a parlé	a vu	

Mini-histoire

D'abord, Robert a fait ses devoirs. Ensuite, il a parlé trois heures au téléphone à Marie-Claire. Après, il a lu une lettre de Marie-Claire... vingt fois! Après ça, il est allé au cinéma et il a vu Marie-Claire... avec un autre garçon! Finalement, il a raté le bus. Robert a passé un très mauvais week-end.

Au téléphone
DEUXIEME ETAPE

CHAPITRE 9

Vocabulaire

répond	est là	attend
lui dit	Vous pouvez lui dire… ?	encore une fois
Je peux parler à Marie-Claire?	bien sûr	Ça ne répond pas.

Mini-histoire

Robert téléphone à Marie-Claire. C'est la mère de Marie-Claire qui répond.
Robert lui dit, «Bonjour. Je peux parler à Marie-Claire?» Sa mère dit que
Marie-Claire est là, mais qu'elle étudie. Robert lui dit, «Vous pouvez lui dire
que j'ai téléphoné?» La mère dit, «Bien sûr!» Robert attend deux heures.
Il téléphone à Marie-Claire encore une fois mais ça ne répond pas. Robert
est triste.

Au téléphone

CHAPITRE 9

TROISIEME ETAPE

Vocabulaire

J'ai un petit problème.

Tu as une minute?

Je t'écoute.

Qu'est-ce que je peux faire?

Ne t'en fais pas.

Mini-histoire

Robert téléphone à son ami Jean-Marc. Robert lui dit, «J'ai un petit problème. Tu as une minute?» Jean-Marc lui répond, «Je t'écoute. Qu'est-ce que je peux faire?» Robert dit, «J'ai téléphoné à Marie-Claire. Elle est là, mais ça ne répond pas.» Jean-Marc lui répond, «Ne t'en fais pas. Elle n'est pas là. Elle écoute des CD avec moi!» Maintenant Robert est très triste!

Teacher Notes

PREMIERE ETAPE

TPRS Gestures

d'abord grab thumb

a fait ses devoirs mime writing in practice workbook

ensuite count to two starting with thumb and grab index finger

a parlé mime talking

après point backwards with thumb

a lu mime reading

est allé indicate going out the door with hand

a vu point to eyes

finalement mime "first, second, third" with fingers and then open hand in chopping motion towards palm to show last

a raté le bus mime chasing bus and waving to driver

a passé un très mauvais week-end hold both thumbs down and frown

Teaching Suggestions

• Give students the definition of **autre** before presenting the story.

• Verbs in the **passé composé** should be followed with the hand "thrown" over the back to indicate past tense.

• Students should have their practice workbooks and pens on their desks for **a fait ses devoirs**.

Additional Vocabulary

épouvantable mime look of horror

très chouette hold both thumbs up and smile

a acheté mime pulling money out of wallet and handing it to someone

a cherché open hand, palm down, to forehead, as if looking/searching for something

DEUXIEME ETAPE

TPRS Gestures

répond mime picking up telephone

lui dit touch lips with fingers and pull fingers away, then point to a student

Je peux parler à Marie-Claire? point to yourself and mime talking with hand

est là index finger points towards something; symbolizes "there"

Vous pouvez lui dire... ? make question mark in air with index finger, mime talking with hand

bien sûr nod head yes

attend fold arms/hands over chest as if waiting and tap foot

encore une fois tap back of hand once with fingertips of other hand; then once again

Ça ne répond pas. mime making telephone call, waiting, and hanging up

Teaching Suggestion

• When presenting expressions used on the telephone, mime punching buttons on the phone before making the gesture.

Additional Vocabulary

Je peux laisser un message? make question mark in air, mime taking notes on a small notepad

C'est occupé. mime dialing phone and then make busy signal sound

TROISIEME ETAPE

TPRS Gestures

J'ai un petit problème. show thumb and index finger almost together to show "a little bit" and scratch temple

Tu as une minute? hold up index finger

Je t'écoute. point to ear

Qu'est-ce que je peux faire? shrug shoulders while extending hands out, palms up

Ne t'en fais pas. throw open hand forward as if saying "Forget about it."

Teaching Suggestions

• Before presenting the story, have students recall what they learned about Robert and Marie-Claire from the previous two **étapes**.

• Have students imagine a different ending to this story. Marie-Claire is not with Jean-Marc, and Jean-Marc offers advice to his friend Robert. Have students use expressions from page 279 of the *Pupil's Edition* in their revised versions.

Additional Vocabulary

Qu'est-ce que tu me conseilles? point to student, make question mark in the air, and point back to self

Oublie-le/-la/-les! point to temples with fingers, then snap fingers

Ça va aller mieux! mime frowning, then curve mouth into a smile with fingers

Dans un magasin de vêtements
PREMIÈRE ÉTAPE

Vocabulaire

ne sait pas quoi mettre   un bracelet   des sandales

porte   mets   un chemisier

un cardigan   un pantalon   une robe

des bottes

Mini-histoire

Lise ne sait pas quoi mettre pour aller à la boum de Daniel. Maintenant,
elle porte un jean, un cardigan, des bottes et un bracelet. Elle demande à sa
mère et à son amie Caroline, «Qu'est-ce que je mets pour aller à la boum?»
Sa mère lui dit, «Pourquoi est-ce que tu ne mets pas ton pantalon blanc, tes
sandales et ton chemisier blanc?» Son amie Caroline dit, «Non, mets une robe
et des sandales.» Lise va à la boum de Daniel. Qu'est-ce qu'elle porte? Un
jean, un cardigan, des bottes et un bracelet!

10 Dans un magasin de vêtements
DEUXIEME ETAPE

Vocabulaire

cherche quelque chose   bleu clair   à rayures

pour aller avec   choisit   à carreaux

nouveau(x)   en jean

Mini-histoire

Jean cherche quelque chose pour aller avec son nouveau jean bleu clair. Il choisit une chemise en jean. Il achète aussi une chemise à rayures et une chemise à carreaux. Jean est très content. Maintenant, il pense, «Il me faut de nouveaux jeans pour aller avec mes chemises!»

CHAPITRE 10 Dans un magasin de vêtements
TROISIEME ETAPE

Vocabulaire

Comment tu trouves… ?   Il/Elle me va?   Il/Elle te plaît… ?

Je le/la/les trouve…   serré(e)   large

moche

Mini-histoire

Brigitte est dans un magasin avec son ami Pedro. Elle lui demande,
«Comment tu trouves cette robe?» Il lui répond, «Je la trouve moche.» Elle
demande, «Il me va, ce pantalon?» Il lui répond, «Je le trouve trop serré.»
Finalement, Brigitte demande, «Il te plaît, ce jean?» Pedro répond, «Je le
trouve trop large.» Brigitte n'aime pas faire les magasins avec Pedro!

Teacher Notes

PREMIERE ETAPE

TPRS Gestures

ne sait pas quoi mettre hold up several articles of clothing to self and pretend to decide what to wear

porte mime putting on several articles of clothing

un cardigan mime buttoning a sweater

des bottes mime putting on boots

un bracelet clasp wrist of one hand with the thumb and middle finger of the other hand

mets same gesture as **porte**

un pantalon put hands on both legs, run hands down from thighs to ankles

des sandales wiggle toes and mime buckling sandals

un chemisier mime putting on a blouse and buttoning buttons

une robe make chopping motion on legs where skirt would end

Teaching Suggestions

• Have students retell the story from a boy's point of view.

• After presenting the story, have students explain when to use **mettre** and when to use **porter**.

Additional Vocabulary

des boucles d'oreilles mime putting on earrings

une ceinture mime buckling belt

DEUXIEME ETAPE

TPRS Gestures

cherche quelque chose mime looking for something

pour aller avec show fingers "walking" together with both hands

nouveau(x) pretend to pull new item out of bag and admire it

bleu clair point to or hold up a piece of light blue construction paper

choisit extend fingers of one hand, palm up, and choose one finger by pulling it, then repeat with another finger

en jean point to jeans or denim shirt

à rayures draw stripes on board or in the air with finger

à carreaux draw checked pattern on board or in the air with finger

Teaching Suggestions

• Give students the definition of **pense** before telling the story.

• You might find it easier to teach patterned clothing if you can find examples to bring in and show to the class. Students could also draw the various patterns on paper.

Additional Vocabulary

bleu foncé point to or hold up a piece of dark blue construction paper

en coton touch or point to article of clothing made of cotton

à fleurs mime smelling a flower, plucking petals

à pois draw polka dots on board or in the air with finger

TROISIEME ETAPE

TPRS Gestures

Comment tu trouves... ? make question mark in air, pretend to hold up item of clothing, and raise eyebrows

Je le/la/les trouve... point to picture of masculine, feminine, or plural clothing items found in a fashion magazine, and give thumbs-up and thumbs-down signs

moche make a disgusted face

Il/Elle me va? make question mark in air, point to clothing item, and raise eyebrows

serré(e) grab arm or waist and squeeze

Il/Elle te plaît... ? make question mark in air, hold up clothing item, and raise eyebrows

large mime pulling up pants at waist because they are too "baggy"

Teaching Suggestions

• When presenting the story, you might use sock puppets to convey the dialogue.

• You might want to further practice **Il me va?** and **Elle me va?** by holding up several articles of clothing of different genders.

• Demonstrate the difference between **je le/la/les trouve...** by using feminine, masculine, and plural clothing items.

Additional Vocabulary

Tu aimes mieux... ? make question mark in air and point to either a pencil or a pen

Vive les vacances!

PREMIERE ETAPE

Vocabulaire

à la montagne   en forêt   faire du bateau
chez ses grands-parents   faire du camping   en France
au bord de la mer

Mini-histoire

Qu'est-ce que Laeticia va faire cet été? Elle ne va pas à la montagne chez ses grands-parents. Elle ne va pas au bord de la mer. Elle ne va pas en forêt. Elle ne va pas faire du camping et elle ne va pas faire du bateau. Elle va étudier le français en France. Elle adore le français!

Vive les vacances!
DEUXIEME ETAPE

Vocabulaire

part
il a pensé à tout
un passeport

un billet de train
un cadeau
un billet d'avion

un appareil-photo
de l'argent
il n'a rien oublié

Mini-histoire

Christian part en vacances. Il a pensé à tout! Son passeport, son billet de
train, un cadeau pour sa grand-mère, son billet d'avion, son appareil-photo
et de l'argent sont dans son sac à dos. Christian est très content parce qu'il
n'a rien oublié. A l'aéroport, il cherche son chocolat, mais il l'a oublié!
Maintenant, il a faim!

Vive les vacances!
TROISIEME ETAPE

Vocabulaire

Tu t'es bien amusé(e)?

C'était chouette.

C'était formidable.

Ça a été.

C'était un véritable cauchemar.

Mini-histoire

Tu as passé un bon été? Tu t'es bien amusé(e)? Pour Claudine, c'était chouette parce qu'elle a fait du camping. Pour Didier, c'était formidable. Il est allé chez son oncle à la campagne. Pour Marie, ça a été. Elle a travaillé au fast-food. Pour Benoît, c'était un véritable cauchemar. Il est allé en vacances avec ses petits cousins!

Teacher Notes

PREMIERE ETAPE
TPRS Gestures

à la montagne trace mountain peaks with finger in the air

chez ses grands-parents make a roof of a house by putting middle fingertips of both hands together

au bord de la mer extend arms and look up at sun/ceiling (to represent lying on the beach at seashore) or make waves with hand

en forêt mime looking up a tall tree

faire du camping mime driving stakes into the ground to put up a tent

faire du bateau mime rowing a boat

en France point to map of France (either in the classroom or on page xxiii of the *Pupil's Edition*)

Teaching Suggestion

- You might change the ending of the story each time you tell it. (**Elle va étudier l'espagnol en Espagne. Elle adore l'espagnol!**) This encourages students to pay attention and also use more vocabulary.

Additional Vocabulary

à la campagne represent countryside in the air by using outstretched hand to show flatness of the countryside

faire de la randonnée mime hiking using a walking stick

faire de la plongée mime diving

faire de la voile blow on open palm of hand in front of face to represent wind blowing against sail

DEUXIEME ETAPE
TPRS Gestures

part use fingers to "walk away/leave" on desk

il a pensé à tout touch both temples of head with index fingers and wave hand over desk to represent everything

un passeport mime stamping a passport

un billet de train use thumb and index finger of one hand to "punch" the other hand

un cadeau mime handing a gift to someone

un billet d'avion mime tearing the top part off an airplane ticket and handing the other part to a passenger

un appareil-photo mime snapping photo

de l'argent rub thumb against other fingers of the same hand

il n'a rien oublié make "time out" sign with hands and shake head no

Teaching Suggestions

- Before you present the story, give students the definition of **l'aéroport**.

- To make the story more real to students, hold up actual items that Christian packed as you retell the story. Then have students use the objects when they retell the story.

- Explain to students that train tickets in France are punched (**composter**) to show that they have been used.

Additional Vocabulary

une valise mime packing and closing suitcase

Bon voyage! wave good-bye and blow kisses

Bonnes vacances! same gesture as **Bon voyage!**

TROISIEME ETAPE
TPRS Gestures

Tu t'es bien amusé(e)? make question mark in air, smile, and point to smiling face

C'était chouette. hold two thumbs up

C'était formidable. give a big smile and nod head yes

Ça a été. have neutral expression on face and use hand to make gesture for "so-so"

C'était un véritable cauchemar. grasp both sides of head quickly and look distressed

Teaching Suggestion

- Have students ask some classmates what they did on vacation, and then have them retell the story with their classmates' experiences.

Additional Vocabulary

Pas mauvais. shrug shoulders slightly

C'était ennuyeux. yawn loudly

French 1 *Allez, viens!,* Chapter 11

En ville
PREMIERE ETAPE

Vocabulaire

la boulangerie	la poste	la pharmacie
l'épicerie	les timbres	des médicaments
la librairie	chez le disquaire	la pâtisserie/les pâtisseries

Mini-histoire

Jean va faire les courses. D'abord, il va à la boulangerie pour acheter du pain et à l'épicerie pour acheter des pommes. Ensuite, il va à la librairie pour acheter des livres et à la poste pour acheter des timbres. Après, il va chez le disquaire pour acheter des CD et à la pharmacie pour acheter des médicaments. Enfin, il est très content : il va à la pâtisserie pour acheter des pâtisseries!

En ville
DEUXIEME ETAPE

Vocabulaire

en bus   en train   Il peut y aller...
à vélo   en voiture   en métro
en avion   en taxi

Mini-histoire

Thomas va à l'école en bus et à l'épicerie à vélo. Il va au Canada en avion, il va à Nice en train et il va chez sa tante en voiture. Il va à la pharmacie en taxi. Et comment est-ce qu'il va à la bibliothèque? Il peut y aller à pied, mais il y va en métro parce que c'est plus rapide. Pourquoi est-ce qu'il veut y aller? Thérèse étudie à la bibliothèque!

En ville
TROISIEME ETAPE

Vocabulaire

prend la rue…   tourne   près de
passe   à gauche   derrière
devant   au coin de la rue   à côté de

Mini-histoire

Janine est à l'école. Elle part à 5:30. Elle prend la rue Lamartine et elle
passe devant la maison de sa grand-mère, mais elle n'y va pas. Elle tourne
à gauche au coin de la rue. Elle est près de la maison de son oncle, mais elle
n'y va pas. Elle passe devant la maison de son amie Nathalie. Nathalie est
derrière la maison, mais Janine n'y va pas. Maintenant elle est devant sa
maison, mais elle n'y va pas. Elle va à l'épicerie à côté de sa maison parce
qu'elle a très faim!

Teacher Notes

PREMIERE ETAPE

TPRS Gestures

la boulangerie mime slicing bread or breaking a baguette

l'épicerie mime holding basket and selecting produce

la librairie put hands together by little fingers to represent a book, then mime paying for something

la poste say **PTT** in French

les timbres mime licking a stamp and putting it on an envelope

chez le disquaire cover both ears with cupped hands to represent headphones

la pharmacie make a cross with index fingers

des médicaments mime taking medicine with a spoon

la pâtisserie/les pâtisseries mime eating a small pastry

Teaching Suggestions

- Tell students that **PTT** (**Postes, Télécommunications et Télédiffusion**) is an acronym for the French postal system.

- Explain to students that a green cross is the symbol for a French pharmacy.

Additional Vocabulary

rendre des livres mime returning books by taking them out of a bag and putting them on table

envoyer des lettres mime opening mailbox and putting in a letter

à la banque mime counting out bills

DEUXIEME ETAPE

TPRS Gestures

en bus mime driving bus

à vélo mime holding onto bicycle handlebars and pedaling feet

en avion pretend to fly with arms extended

en train mime pulling train whistle and saying "Choo Choo"

en voiture mime driving car

en taxi mime hailing a taxi

Il peut y aller... make fists with both hands and hold in front of you, then lower the fists while you nod and smile

en métro mime holding on to bar or strap to keep one's balance in a subway car

Teaching Suggestions

- Give students the meaning of **rapide** before presenting the story.

- You might have students retell the story using different forms of transportation to get to the various destinations. Encourage students to be as creative as possible in their versions.

Additional Vocabulary

en bateau mime rowing and adjusting sails

TROISIEME ETAPE

TPRS Gestures

prend la rue... trace the side of desk with index finger to represent walking down a street

passe place tip of index finger from one hand on desk and use other index finger to pass by it

devant put open hand in front of desk

tourne walk and turn

à gauche put open hand to the left of desk

au coin de la rue trace the corner of desk with index finger

près de place tips of index fingers close to one another, but not touching

derrière put open hand behind desk

à côté de point to the desk next to you

Teaching Suggestions

- Give students the definition of **maison** before telling the story.

- Before telling the story, make sure students understand what you consider to be the "front" and "back" of the desk, so you are all working from the same perspective.

- Have students refer to the map on page 372 of the *Pupil's Edition* if you have them invent another story using directions.

- Have students retell and act out the story with certain areas of the classroom designated as locations.

Additional Vocabulary

à droite put open hand to the right of desk

loin de place tips of index fingers far apart

jusqu'au prochain feu rouge put open hand out to indicate "stop"